Piano • Vocal • Guitar

Songs Of Love

S0-CFL-059

ISBN 0-7935-3806-8

HAL•LEONARD
CORPORATION
7777 W. BLUEMOUND RD. P.O. BOX 13819 MILWAUKEE, WI 53213

Copyright © 1994 by HAL LEONARD CORPORATION
International Copyright Secured All Rights Reserved

For all works contained herein:
Unauthorized copying, arranging, adapting, recording or public performance is an infringement of copyright.
Infringers are liable under the law.

Songs Of Love

All The Things You Are.............................4

Always...7

Always On My Mind...............................12

And So It Goes 15

Call Me Irresponsible...........................20

Can You Feel The Love Tonight 24

Can't Smile Without You 28

Candy 34

Danke Schoen....................................37

Dearly Beloved 40

Dream A Little Dream Of Me......................43

Easy To Love
(a/k/a You'd Be So Easy To Love) 46

Falling In Love With Love.......................49

A Fine Romance 52

Friends & Lovers (Both To Each Other).......60

Have I Told You Lately 64

How Deep Is The Ocean
(How High Is The Sky)...........................69

I Can't Give You Anything But Love 72

I Swear...75

I Want You To Want Me 80

I Wish You Love 86

If...90

If We Only Have Love 93

Just In Time....................................96

Just Once 98

Let It Be Me (Je T'appartiens)................104

Long And Winding Road, The 106

Love Is A Simple Thing 110

Love Of A Lifetime 113

Love Takes Time 120

Magic Touch, (You've Got) The 124

Misty 127

My Funny Valentine 130

On My Word Of Honor 132

P.S. I Love You 135

Power Of Love, The 138

Romeo And Juliet (Love Theme)................144

Roses Are Red (My Love)........................147

Saving All My Love For You 150

Share Your Love With Me 154

She Believes In Me 162

Soft Lights And Sweet Music 168

Something 172

Somewhere In Time..............................176

(You're My) Soul And Inspiration 178

Tears In Heaven 157

There's A Kind Of Hush
(All Over The World) 182

Things We Did Last Summer, The 186

This Will Be (An Everlasting Love) 192

To Be With You 196

Truly 202

Try To Remember 206

Way We Were, The 189

What The World Needs Now Is Love 208

When I Fall In Love 220

Whole New World, A (Aladdin's Theme)..211

You Give Good Love 222

You're The Inspiration.........................227

ALL THE THINGS YOU ARE
(From "VERY WARM FOR MAY")

Lyrics by OSCAR HAMMERSTEIN II
Music by JEROME KERN

Copyright © 1939 PolyGram International Publishing, Inc.
Copyright Renewed
International Copyright Secured   All Rights Reserved

ALWAYS

Words and Music by
IRVING BERLIN

© Copyright 1925 by Irving Berlin
Copyright Renewed
International Copyright Secured   All Rights Reserved

now that I've found you at last, _____
then will my found love lin - ger on. _____

I'll be lov - ing you, al - ways _____

with a love that's true,

al - ways _____ When the things you've

ALWAYS ON MY MIND

Words and Music by WAYNE THOMPSON,
MARK JAMES and JOHNNY CHRISTOPHER

© 1971, 1979 SCREEN GEMS-EMI MUSIC INC. and BUDDE SONGS INC.
All Rights Controlled and Administered by SCREEN GEMS-EMI MUSIC INC.
All Rights Reserved   International Copyright Secured   Used by Permission

14

AND SO IT GOES

Words and Music by
BILLY JOEL

Slow Ballad, with much rubato

© 1983 JOEL SONGS
All Rights Controlled and Administered by EMI BLACKWOOD MUSIC INC.
All Rights Reserved   International Copyright Secured   Used by Permission

too. And you can have this heart to break.

And so it goes, and so it goes,

and you're the on - ly one who knows.

CALL ME IRRESPONSIBLE

(From The Paramount Picture "PAPA'S DELICATE CONDITION")

Words by SAMMY CAHN
Music by JAMES VAN HEUSEN

Copyright © 1962, 1963 (Renewed 1990, 1991) by Paramount Music Corporation
International Copyright Secured   All Rights Reserved

CAN YOU FEEL THE LOVE TONIGHT

(From Walt Disney Pictures' "THE LION KING")

Music by ELTON JOHN
Lyrics by TIM RICE

© 1994 Wonderland Music Company, Inc.
International Copyright Secured   All Rights Reserved

CAN'T SMILE WITHOUT YOU

Words and Music by CHRIS ARNOLD,
DAVID MARTIN and GEOFF MORROW

Copyright © 1975 Dick James Music Limited
All Rights for the United States and Canada Administered by Songs Of PolyGram International, Inc.
International Copyright Secured   All Rights Reserved

CANDY

Words and Music by MACK DAVID,
JOAN WHITNEY and ALEX KRAMER

Copyright © 1944 PolyGram International Publishing, Inc. and Bourne Co.
Copyright Renewed
International Copyright Secured   All Rights Reserved

DANKE SCHOEN

Lyrics by KURT SCHWABACH and MILT GABLER
Music by BERT KAEMPFERT

© 1962 (Renewed 1990) TONIKA-VERLAG HORST BUSSOW
All Rights Controlled and Administered by SCREEN GEMS-EMI MUSIC INC.
All Rights Reserved   International Copyright Secured   Used by Permission

DEARLY BELOVED
(From "YOU WERE NEVER LOVELIER")

Music by JEROME KERN
Words by JOHNNY MERCER

Copyright © 1942 PolyGram International Publishing, Inc.
Copyright Renewed
International Copyright Secured   All Rights Reserved

Refrain-Andante cantabile, ma ben ritmato

DREAM A LITTLE DREAM OF ME

Words by GUS KAHN
Music by WILBUR SCHWANDT and FABIAN ANDREE

TRO - © Copyright 1930 (Renewed) and 1931 (Renewed) Essex Music, Inc., Words and Music, Inc., New York, NY,
Don Swan Publications, Miami, FL and Gilbert Keyes Music, Hollywood, CA
International Copyright Secured
All Rights Reserved Including Public Performance For Profit
Used by Permission

EASY TO LOVE
(a/k/a YOU'D BE SO EASY TO LOVE)
(From "BORN TO DANCE")

Words and Music by
COLE PORTER

I know too well that I'm ___ just wast-ing pre-cious time in

think-ing such a thing could be, That you ___ could ev-er care for me,

Copyright © 1936 by Chappell & Co.
Copyright Renewed, Assigned to John F. Wharton, Trustee of the Cole Porter Musical and Literary Property Trusts
Chappell & Co. owner of publication and allied rights throughout the world
International Copyright Secured   All Rights Reserved

48

FALLING IN LOVE WITH LOVE

(From "THE BOYS FROM SYRACUSE")

Words by LORENZ HART
Music by RICHARD RODGERS

Copyright © 1938 by Chappell & Co.
Copyright Renewed
All Rights on behalf of The Estate Of Lorenz Hart Administered by WB Music Corp.
International Copyright Secured   All Rights Reserved

A FINE ROMANCE

(From "SWING TIME")

Words by DOROTHY FIELDS
Music by JEROME KERN

Copyright © 1936 PolyGram International Publishing, Inc. and Aldi Music (c/o The Songwriters Guild Of America)
Copyright Renewed
International Copyright Secured   All Rights Reserved

58

FRIENDS & LOVERS
(BOTH TO EACH OTHER)

Words and Music by PAUL GORDON
and JAY GRUSKA

Medium Ballad

What would you say if I told you, I've al - ways
Yes, it's a chance that we're tak - ing, and some - bod - y's

© 1982, 1986 COLGEMS-EMI MUSIC INC., WB MUSIC CORP. and FRENCH SURF MUSIC
All Rights on behalf of FRENCH SURF MUSIC Administered by WB MUSIC CORP.
All Rights Reserved   International Copyright Secured   Used by Permission

HAVE I TOLD YOU LATELY

Words and Music by
VAN MORRISON

Slowly, with expression

Have I told ___ you late-ly that I love you? Have I

told you there's no one else ___ a-bove ___ you?

Fill my heart ___ with glad-ness, take a-way all ___ my sad-ness,

Copyright © 1989 Caledonia Publishing Ltd.
All Rights for the United States and Canada Administered by Songs Of PolyGram International, Inc.
International Copyright Secured   All Rights Reserved

66

HOW DEEP IS THE OCEAN
(HOW HIGH IS THE SKY)

Words and Music by
IRVING BERLIN

© Copyright 1932 by Irving Berlin
Copyright Renewed
International Copyright Secured   All Rights Reserved

I CAN'T GIVE YOU ANYTHING BUT LOVE

(From "BLACKBIRDS OF 1928")

Words by DOROTHY FIELDS
Music by JIMMY McHUGH

Copyright © 1928 ALDI MUSIC and IRENEADELE MUSIC
Copyright Renewed
Pursuant to Sections 304(c) and 401(b) of the U.S. Copyright Law.
International Copyright Secured   All Rights Reserved

I SWEAR

Words and Music by FRANK J. MYERS
and GARY BAKER

I see the ques - tions in___ your eyes;___   I know what's weigh -
I'll give you ev - 'ry - thing___ I can;___   I'll build your dreams _

Copyright © 1989 Morganactive Songs, Inc. (c/o Morgan Music Group, Inc.) and Rick Hall Music, Inc.
International Copyright Secured   All Rights Reserved

I WANT YOU TO WANT ME

Words and Music by
RICK NIELSEN

Bright Two-Beat

I want you to want me.

I need you to need me.

I'd

© 1977, 1978 SCREEN GEMS-EMI MUSIC INC. and ADULT MUSIC
All Rights Controlled and Administered by SCREEN GEMS-EMI MUSIC INC.
All Rights Reserved   International Copyright Secured   Used by Permission

ad lib. guitar solo

Feel-in' all a - lone with-out a friend you know you feel like dy - in'._____

_____ Oh, Did - n't I, did - n't, I did - n't I see you

I WISH YOU LOVE

English Lyric by ALBERT A. BEACH
Music by CHARLES TRENET

© Copyright 1946, 1955 EDITIONS SALABERT
Copyright Renewed
All Rights in the USA and Canada Controlled and Administered by MCA MUSIC PUBLISHING, A Division of MCA INC.
International Copyright Secured   All Rights Reserved

MCA music publishing

IF

Words and Music by
DAVID GATES

Moderately, with feeling

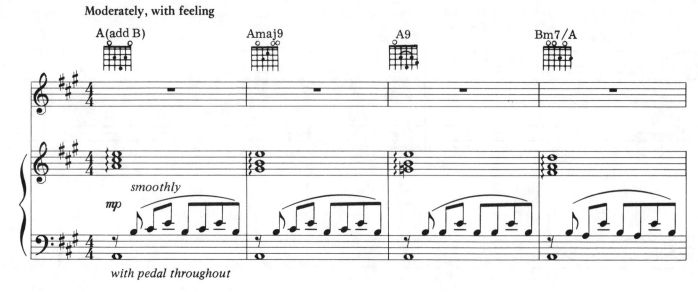

smoothly

with pedal throughout

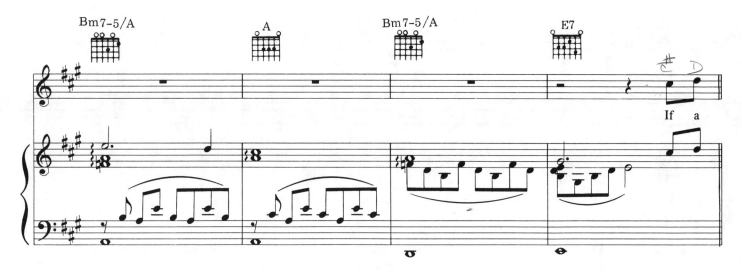

If a

pic - ture paints a thou - sand words,___ then why___ can't I___ paint
man could be two plac - es at___ one time,___ I'd be___ with

© 1971 COLGEMS-EMI MUSIC INC.
All Rights Reserved International Copyright Secured Used by Permission

IF WE ONLY HAVE LOVE

English Lyrics by MORT SHUMAN and ERIC BLAU
Original French Lyrics and Music by JACQUES BREL

1. If We On-ly Have Love, then to-mor-row will dawn;
2. If We On-ly Have Love, we can reach those in pain;

And the days of our years will rise on that morn. If We On-ly Have Love,
We can heal all our wounds, we can use our own names. If We On-ly Have Love,

Copyright © 1968 by Unichappell Music Inc.
International Copyright Secured   All Rights Reserved

JUST IN TIME
(From "BELLS ARE RINGING")

Words by BETTY COMDEN and ADOLPH GREEN
Music by JULE STYNE

Copyright © 1956 by Betty Comden, Adolph Green and Jule Styne
Copyright Renewed
Stratford Music Corporation, owner of publication and allied rights throughout the world
Chappell & Co., Administrator
International Copyright Secured   All Rights Reserved

JUST ONCE

Words by CYNTHIA WEIL
Music by BARRY MANN

© 1981 ATV MUSIC CORP. and MANN & WEIL SONGS, INC.
All Rights Controlled and Administered by EMI BLACKWOOD MUSIC INC. under license from ATV MUSIC CORP.
All Rights Reserved   International Copyright Secured   Used by Permission

LET IT BE ME
(JE T'APPARTIENS)

English Words by MANN CURTIS
French Words by PIERRE DeLANOE
Music by GILBERT BECAUD

© Copyright 1955, 1957, 1960 by FRANCE MUSIC CO.
Copyright Renewed
All Rights in the USA and Canada Controlled and Administered by MCA MUSIC PUBLISHING, A Division of MCA INC.
International Copyright Secured   All Rights Reserved
MCA music publishing

THE LONG AND WINDING ROAD

Words and Music by JOHN LENNON
and PAUL McCARTNEY

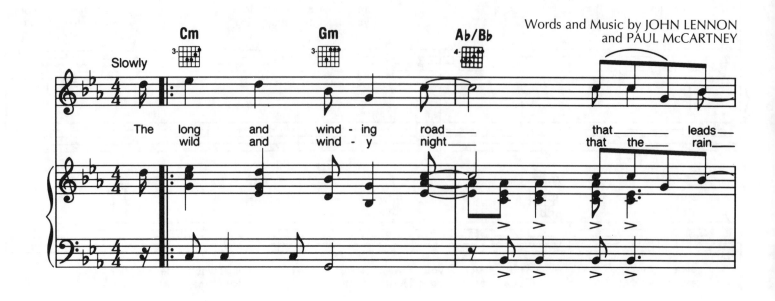

The long and wind-ing road____ that the leads____
wild and wind-y night____ that the rain____

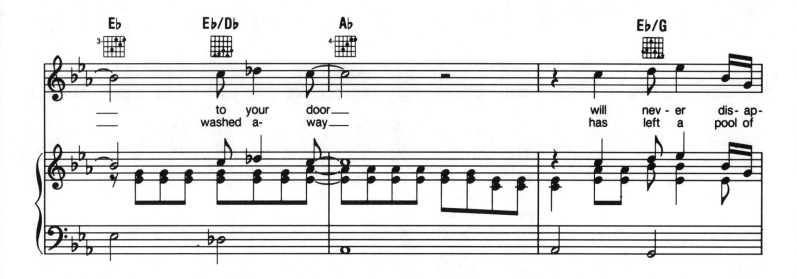

____ to your door____ will nev-er dis-ap-
____ washed a-way has left a pool of

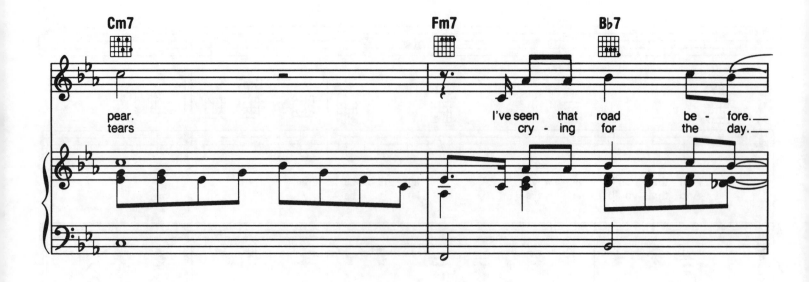

pear. I've seen that road be-fore.____
tears cry-ing for the day.____

© 1970 NORTHERN SONGS LTD.
All Rights Controlled and Administered by EMI BLACKWOOD MUSIC INC. under license from ATV MUSIC CORP. (MACLEN MUSIC)
All Rights Reserved   International Copyright Secured   Used by Permission

LOVE IS A SIMPLE THING

Words by JUNE CARROLL
Music by ARTHUR SIEGEL

Copyright © 1952 by Chappell & Co.
Copyright Renewed
International Copyright Secured   All Rights Reserved

LOVE OF A LIFETIME

Words and Music by BILL LEVERTY
and CARL SNARE

Copyright © 1990 Sony Tunes Inc. and Wocka Wocka Music
All Rights Administered by Sony Music Publishing, 8 Music Square West, Nashville, TN 37203
International Copyright Secured   All Rights Reserved

115

LOVE TAKES TIME

Words and Music by MARIAH CAREY
and BEN MARGULIES

Copyright © 1990 Vision Of Love Songs, Inc. and Been Jammin' Music
All Rights on behalf of Vision Of Love Songs, Inc. Administered by Sony Music Publishing, 8 Music Square West, Nashville, TN 37203
International Copyright Secured   All Rights Reserved

(YOU'VE GOT)
THE MAGIC TOUCH

Words and Music by
BUCK RAM

Copyright © 1956 All Nations Music and AMC, Inc.
Copyright Renewed 1984
International Copyright Secured All Rights Reserved

MISTY

Words by JOHNNY BURKE
Music by ERROLL GARNER

© 1954, 1955 REGANESQUE MUSIC, MARKE MUSIC PUBLISHING CO., INC., LIMERICK MUSIC CORP., TIMO-CO MUSIC and OCTAVE MUSIC PUBLISHING CORP.
Copyright Renewed
All rights on behalf of OCTAVE MUSIC PUBLISHING CORP. administered by WB MUSIC CORP.
All Rights Reserved

MY FUNNY VALENTINE

(From "BABES IN ARMS")

Words by LORENZ HART
Music by RICHARD RODGERS

Copyright © 1937 by Chappell & Co.
Copyright Renewed, Assigned to Williamson Music and The Estate Of Lorenz Hart
All Rights on behalf of The Estate Of Lorenz Hart Administered by WB Music Corp.
International Copyright Secured   All Rights Reserved

ON MY WORD OF HONOR

Words and Music by KATHERINE HARRISON
and JEAN MILES

Copyright © 1957 (Renewed 1985) Music Of The World, Argo Music, Inc. and Up The Block Music
International Copyright Secured   All Rights Reserved

P.S. I LOVE YOU

Words by JOHNNY MERCER
Music by GORDON JENKINS

What is there to write, what is there to say? Same things hap-pen ev-'ry

day; Not a thing to write, not a thing to say,

So I take my pen in hand and start the same old way. ___

© Copyright 1934 by LA SALLE MUSIC PUBLISHERS INC.
Copyright Renewed, Assigned to MCA MUSIC PUBLISHING, A Division of MCA INC. and WB MUSIC CORP.
International Copyright Secured   All Rights Reserved
MCA music publishing

THE POWER OF LOVE

Words by MARY SUSAN APPLEGATE and JENNIFER RUSH
Music by CANDY DEROUGE and GUNTHER MENDE

© 1986 EMI SONGS MUSIKVERLAG GMBH
All Rights for the U.S.A. and Canada Controlled and Administered by EMI APRIL MUSIC INC.
All Rights Reserved International Copyright Secured Used by Permission

ROMEO AND JULIET
(LOVE THEME)
(From The Paramount Picture "ROMEO AND JULIET")

By NINO ROTA

Copyright © 1968 by Famous Music Corporation
International Copyright Secured   All Rights Reserved

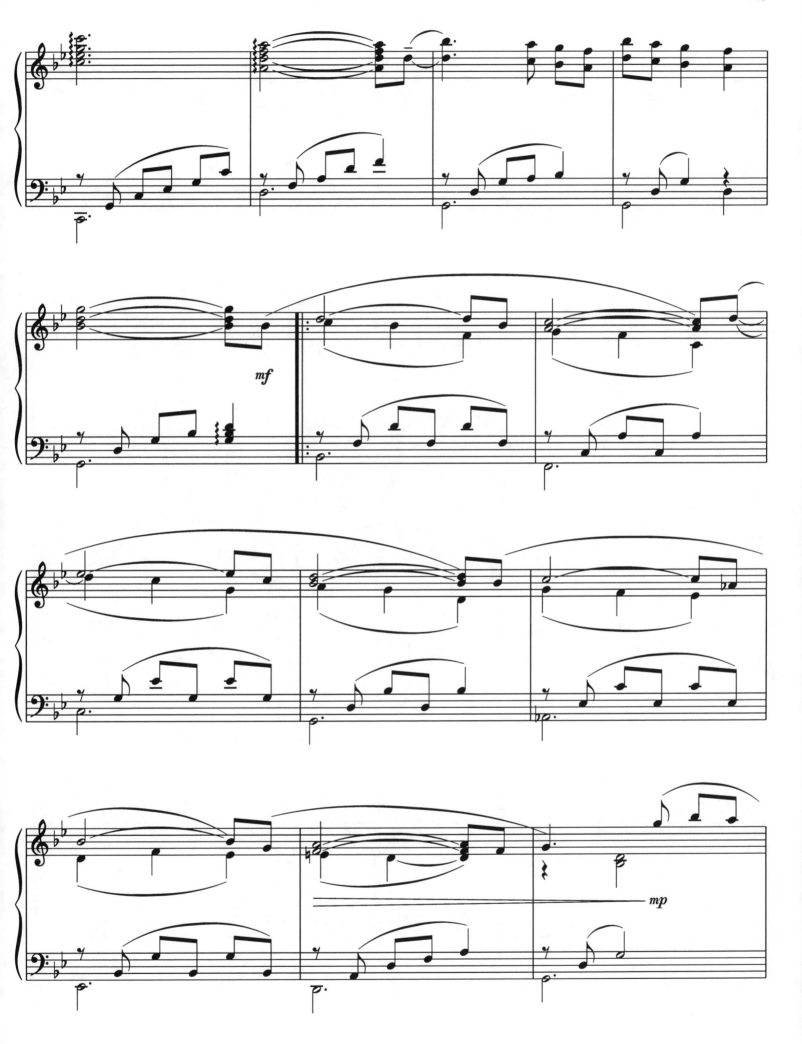

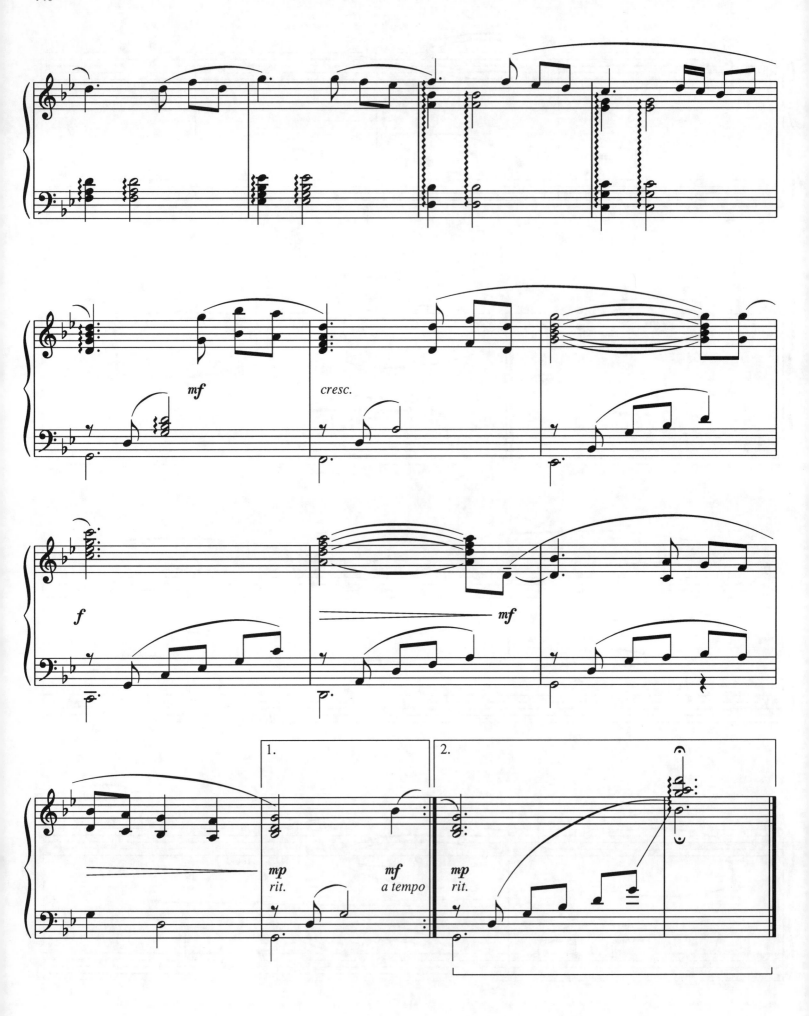

ROSES ARE RED
(MY LOVE)

Words and Music by AL BYRON
and PAUL EVANS

Copyright © 1961 United Artists Music Co., Inc.
Copyright Renewed, Assigned to Port Music, Inc. and Iyamusic Publishing for the United States
International Copyright Secured   All Rights Reserved

148

SAVING ALL MY LOVE FOR YOU

Words by GERRY GOFFIN
Music by MICHAEL MASSER

© 1978 SCREEN GEMS-EMI MUSIC INC., LAUREN-WESLEY MUSIC INC. and PRINCE STREET MUSIC
All Rights for LAUREN-WESLEY MUSIC INC. Controlled and Administered by SCREEN GEMS-EMI MUSIC INC.
All Rights Reserved   International Copyright Secured   Used by Permission

SHARE YOUR LOVE WITH ME

Words and Music by DEADRIC MALONE
and AL BRAGGS

© Copyright 1963, 1981 by MUSIC CORPORATION OF AMERICA, INC.
Copyright Renewed
International Copyright Secured   All Rights Reserved
MCA music publishing

TEARS IN HEAVEN

Words and Music by ERIC CLAPTON
and WILL JENNINGS

Copyright © 1991 by EC Music Limited and Blue Sky Rider Songs
All Rights for EC Music Limited Administered by Unichappell Music Inc.
International Copyright Secured   All Rights Reserved

158

Be - yond   the   door ___

there's peace, I'm sure. __

SHE BELIEVES IN ME

Words and Music by
STEVE GIBB

Copyright © 1977 PolyGram International Publishing, Inc.
International Copyright Secured   All Rights Reserved

SOFT LIGHTS AND SWEET MUSIC
(From The Stage Production "FACE THE MUSIC")

Words and Music by
IRVING BERLIN

© Copyright 1931 by Irving Berlin
Copyright Renewed
International Copyright Secured   All Rights Reserved

SOMETHING

Words and Music by
GEORGE HARRISON

© 1969 HARRISONGS LTD.
International Copyright Secured   All Rights Reserved

SOMEWHERE IN TIME
(From "SOMEWHERE IN TIME")

By JOHN BARRY

© Copyright 1980 by DUCHESS MUSIC CORPORATION
DUCHESS MUSIC CORPORATION is an MCA company
International Copyright Secured   All Rights Reserved

MCA music publishing

8va

(YOU'RE MY)
SOUL AND INSPIRATION

Words and Music by BARRY MANN
and CYNTHIA WEIL

© 1966 (Renewed 1994) SCREEN GEMS-EMI MUSIC INC.
All Rights Reserved   International Copyright Secured   Used by Permission

THERE'S A KIND OF HUSH
(ALL OVER THE WORLD)

Words and Music by LES REED
and GEOFF STEPHENS

Moderately, with a steady beat

There's a kind of hush all o-ver the world to-night, all o-ver the world you can hear the sounds of lov-ers in love.

© 1966 (Renewed 1994) DONNA MUSIC LTD.
All Rights Controlled and Administered by GLENWOOD MUSIC CORP.
All Rights Reserved   International Copyright Secured   Used by Permission

THE THINGS WE DID LAST SUMMER

Words and Music by SAMMY CAHN
and JULE STYNE

Copyright © 1946 by Cahn Music Co. and Producers Music Publishing Co.
Copyright Renewed
All Rights on behalf of Producers Music Publishing Co. Administered by Chappell & Co.
All Rights on behalf of Cahn Music Co. Administered by WB Music Corp.
International Copyright Secured   All Rights Reserved

THE WAY WE WERE

(From The Motion Picture "THE WAY WE WERE")

Words by ALAN and MARILYN BERGMAN
Music by MARVIN HAMLISCH

© 1973 COLGEMS-EMI MUSIC INC.
All Rights Reserved   International Copyright Secured   Used by Permission

THIS WILL BE
(AN EVERLASTING LOVE)

Words and Music by MARVIN YANCY
and CHUCK JACKSON

Copyright © 1975 by Jay's Enterprises, Inc. and Chappell & Co.
All Rights Administered by Chappell & Co.
International Copyright Secured   All Rights Reserved

TO BE WITH YOU

Words and Music by ERIC MARTIN
and DAVID GRAHAME

© 1991 EMI APRIL MUSIC INC., DOG TURNER MUSIC and ERIC MARTIN SONGS
All Rights Controlled and Administered by EMI APRIL MUSIC INC.
All Rights Reserved   International Copyright Secured   Used By Permission

TRULY

Words and Music by
LIONEL RICHIE

Copyright © 1982 Brockman Music (ASCAP)
International Copyright Secured   All Rights Reserved

TRY TO REMEMBER
(From "THE FANTASTICKS")

Words by TOM JONES
Music by HARVEY SCHMIDT

Copyright © 1960 by Tom Jones and Harvey Schmidt
Copyright Renewed
Chappell & Co. owner of publication and allied rights throughout the world
International Copyright Secured   All Rights Reserved

WHAT THE WORLD NEEDS NOW IS LOVE

Lyric by HAL DAVID
Music by BURT BACHARACH

Copyright © 1965 Blue Seas Music, Inc. and Casa David
Copyright Renewed
International Copyright Secured   All Rights Reserved

A WHOLE NEW WORLD
(ALADDIN'S THEME)
(From Walt Disney's "ALADDIN")

Music by ALAN MENKEN
Lyrics by TIM RICE

Male: I can show you the world,
I can o - pen your eyes

shin - ing, shim - mer - ing, splen - did.
take you won - der by won - der

Tell me, prin - cess, now
o - ver, side - ways and

when did you last let your heart de - cide?
un - der on a

© 1992 Wonderland Music Company, Inc. and Walt Disney Music Company
International Copyright Secured   All Rights Reserved

Let me share _____ this whole new world_ with you. _____

A whole new world. _

A whole new

WHEN I FALL IN LOVE

Words by EDWARD HEYMAN
Music by VICTOR YOUNG

Copyright © 1952 by Chappell & Co. and Intersong U.S.A., Inc.
Copyright Renewed
International Copyright Secured   All Rights Reserved

YOU GIVE GOOD LOVE

Words and Music by
LA FORREST "LA LA" COPE

© Copyright 1985 by MCA MUSIC PUBLISHING, A Division of MCA INC. and LITTLE TANYA MUSIC
All Rights Controlled and Administered by MCA MUSIC PUBLISHING, A Division of MCA INC.
International Copyright Secured   All Rights Reserved

MCA music publishing

YOU'RE THE INSPIRATION

Words and Music by PETER CETERA
and DAVID FOSTER

Copyright © 1984 by BMG Songs, Inc. and Foster Frees Music, Inc.
International Copyright Secured   All Rights Reserved

Additional Lyrics

2. And I know (yes, I know)
   That it's plain to see
   We're so in love when we're together.
   Now I know (now I know)
   That I need you here with me
   From tonight until the end of time.
   You should know everywhere I go;
   Always on my mind, you're in my heart, in my soul.
   (To Chorus:)